Tropical Fish Aquariums Guide For Beginners

Karl McCullough

Tropical Fish Aquariums Guide For Beginners
by Karl McCullough

ISBN 978-1-926917-18-4

Printed in the United States of America

Copyright © 2010 Psylon Press

INTRODUCTION

Adding a tropical fish aquarium to your home is a wonderful way to enjoy the beauty of the ocean right within the comforts of your own home. A tropical fish aquarium featuring a variety of brilliantly colored fish and surrounded by vivid vegetation can be not only beautiful but also very relaxing and calming as well.

Before you start your tropical fish aquarium, it is important to have some relevant information at your disposal. Tropical fish are beautiful, but there are some things that you need to know to ensure that your fish remain beautiful and healthy for a long time.

In this guide we will discuss the basic information that you need to know how to choose the right aquarium for your needs along with various accessories and even how to choose from among the many different species of fish that are available. This is an important step as there are some types of tropical fish that have far more demands in order to remain healthy than others.

Maintaining a tropical fish aquarium can be a relaxing and rewarding hobby when you have the right information at your fingertips. This guide will provide you with all of the information you need to know to get your aquarium underway, even if you happen to be a novice at keeping fish. We will cover various topics such as how to get your aquarium initially set up as well as various illnesses that you should be on the lookout for in your fish and how to treat them.

In addition, you will find a daily, weekly and monthly maintenance guide that will walk you through the steps of properly maintaining your aquarium to achieve the optimal results.

Let's get started!

GETTING STARTED

In this chapter we are going to be discussing some of the basics that you will need to understand in order to appropriately set up your aquarium so it will be ready to welcome your fish.

How to Set up an Aquarium

There are many different types and styles of aquariums available on the market today, but they all have one thing in common; they are suitable for sustaining fish as well as other types of aquatic life. There are a few factors that should be taken into consideration when buying an aquarium to experience the best results. You should keep in mind that the process of actually setting up your aquarium so that it will be ready for your fish could take as much as a month. While that may seem like a long time, especially if you are anxious to get started, it should be kept in mind that it is much better to take the time to get your aquarium set up correctly now than to find out later that you rushed through the process and you fish suffered as a result.

When buying your aquarium you need to ask yourself a few questions. For example, how much time are you will to dedicate on caring for your aquarium and fish? What type of aquarium do you wish to buy? Where is the ideal location in your home for your aquarium? What types of fish would you like to keep?

You will also need to purchase some equipment and supplies for your aquarium. Some basic equipment that will be needed includes:

- Aquarium tank
- Aquarium stand
- Hood
- Lighting equipment
- Air pump
- Heater
- Thermometer
- Filters
- Gravel
- Decorations
- Maintenance equipment such as siphon tube, scrubber, etc.

Choosing a Location for your Aquarium

Before you actually buy your aquarium you should consider the amount of free space you have available to position your aquarium. Keep in mind that an aquarium should never be placed within direct sunlight. Also, you should not place your aquarium anywhere near any cooling or heating surface. Sunlight as well as heating and cooling surfaces can cause dangerous changes within the water temperature. You should also take care to situate your aquarium away from any appliances or machines that will cause a lot of noise or vibration as this can cause your fish to be stressed.

Most people find that positioning the aquarium in an area where they can easily dispose of dirty water and access fresh water for the tank is more convenient. Remember that you will need to change the water at least once a month, if not once per week, so try to choose a location where you can do this is the easiest and most convenient manner possible.

If you have young children, you may want to choose an area of the home where the aquarium will be kept away from a lot of activity. You certainly do not want your children accidentally falling into the aquarium and becoming injured or causing your fish to be stressed.

Finally, you may wish to take into consideration where your fish aquarium will look best in your home, factoring in your existing décor and how well it will look with your aquarium.

Selecting an Aquarium

There are many different options when it comes to choosing the size of your aquarium as there is a variety of different shapes as well as sizes available. At a minimum, you should consider selecting an aquarium that is at least 10 gallons due to the fact that it can much more difficult to maintain a smaller aquarium. This is because the waste build up in a smaller tank tends to occur more rapidly, requiring you to change the water more frequently. In addition, changes within the water chemistry and/or the temperature also tend to occur more rapidly in a smaller tank and this can be dangerous for your fish.

If you have enough space to accommodate it, you may wish to consider getting a 30 gallon tank as this will provide you with additional space for more fish as well as easier maintenance.

When it comes to size, there are also many options to choose from here as well. For example, you can choose the traditional hexagonal shape or a cylindrical shape. When choosing the shape, consider practical matters such as how easy it will be for you to clean the tank. In addition, you should consider the depth of the tank and remember that aquariums which are very deep can also be more difficult to clean. Deep tanks also often experience problems with poor light penetration, which can make it difficult for plants to thrive.

Glass or Acrylic?

Another decision that will need to be made is whether you wish to use a glass or an acrylic aquarium. A glass tank will be less expensive and will not be as prone to being scratched as an acrylic tank. Glass tanks are also much stronger and durable, capable of lasting for many years. Perhaps the only real drawback to a glass aquarium is that it is heavier than an acrylic tank.

Acrylic tanks offer the benefit of being clearer over glass and often offer better insulation, which means that you can get by with using a smaller heating to maintain the proper water temperature. Of course, it should be kept in mind that acrylic does tend to scratch more easily and can only be cleaned by using specialty equipment. Price can also be a factor when it comes to acrylic, which is typically more expensive than glass.

Positioning your Aquarium

After you have selected the aquarium that will best suit your needs, the next step is to position it in the correct location. Before you actually do that you should take the time to inspect it for any possible scratches as well as to test it to ensure there are no leaks.

Make sure that you have a hood for your aquarium that will fit tightly over the top. It is never a good idea to have an open aquarium, as it will cause more water to evaporate as a result of heat and sunlight and this can cause the water to become more easily contaminated. Also, if you have an open aquarium, there is a greater chance that some of your fish might actually jump out of the water.

Lighting

Lighting is an essential for your aquarium. Most hoods today have an incandescent or fluorescent light. The best option is a fluorescent bulb because it will burn cooler and not affect the water temperature. In addition, they tend to use less electricity. A fluorescent bulb is more expensive than an incandescent bulb, but the benefits far outweigh the cost difference.

Different sizes of bulbs are available, so you will need to make sure that you have the correct size for your tank.

Heating

A water heater will ensure that the water in your tank is maintained at a consistent temperature, which is important for the health of your fish. The higher the wattage, the more heat the heater can generate. Keep in mind that a larger aquarium will generally require more heat than a smaller aquarium simply because there is more water that must be heated. One option is a heater that can be immersed into the water. This type is fairly easy to read. You can also use a heater that is fully submersible and which can be affixed to the back of the tank, but you will need to take care when taking readings with this type of heater or you could easily cause it to crack.

Only fish such as goldfish which can survive in cold water should be kept in an aquarium without a heart. Most fish simply are not able to tolerate fluctuations within water temperature and eventually will die.

Filtration

You will also need filtration for your aquarium. There are three different types of filtration that can be used in an aquarium. They are:
- Chemical
- Mechanical
- Biological

Mechanical Filtration

Water is passed through a screen or thin sponge in mechanical filtration to help remove debris from the water. The amount of debris as well as the time that is required for it to be filtered from the water will depend upon the quality of the material that is used. Over time, such filters can become clogged and will need to be cleaned to function properly.

Chemical Filtration

Water is passed through an activated carbon in chemical filtration. The carbon assists in making the water clear while also removing possible harmful substances from the water. This type of filtration is best for removing particles that may have been dissolved in the water and thus cannot be removed through the use of mechanical filters.

Biological Filtration

This type of filter utilizes bacteria that actually live on the gravel in the tank or on the surface of the glass in order to break down any harmful substances that may be in the water. It is most effective in reducing toxic waste. In a healthy aquarium, biological filtration takes place naturally.

Air Pumps

When air bubbles rise to the surface of your aquarium they assist in aerating the water as well as detoxifying it. The aeration helps to add oxygen to the water, which can prevent your fish from being harmed by low oxygen levels. If you choose to use an under gravel filtration system, an air pump will help your filter to work better.

Aquarium Decor

When you first step up your new aquarium, you will most like want to add some décor. This will not only make your aquarium more visually appealing but it will also help to create a more natural environment for your fish. There are many different types of decorations that are safe and suitable for aquariums.

The main focus when choosing décor for your aquarium is to ensure that any equipment is securely hidden so that your aquarium will benefit from a more natural look. One option that you can choose is a commercial backdrop that simulates plants, water, etc. Such backdrops can help your fish to feel more secure while also improving the look of your aquarium. Some fish do actually tend to feel shy if they are completely exposed so adding a backdrop can help to solve that problem.

You can also add a substrate to the bottom of your aquarium such as pebbles, sand, etc. This makes for a beautiful addition to your tank but can also help you in buffering the water and ensuring it maintains the proper pH. In addition, substrates can be used for more securely anchoring plants and other décor.

If this is to be your first aquarium, you may find it best to use a natural color gravel that is non-coated. Be sure to exercise care when choosing the size of the pebbles or grave to make sure that the water can flow freely through the under gravel filtration. Sand is not always the best option for beginners due to the fact that it can reduce aeration and water flow.

There are also many other options that can be used to improve the look of your aquarium, such as plants and rock formations.

Plants

Many people choose to use real plants and vegetation in their aquariums. A natural aquarium is a type of aquarium that has only natural plants mixed in with a selection of healthy fish. Plants and fish do tend to do well within the same habitat because they are complimentary. Plants produce the oxygen during photosynthesis that are needed by fish. The fish, in turn, release nitrogenous waste that is used by the plants. Plants also provide many other benefits to a healthy aquarium, including shade and a nesting place for the numerous microorganisms that are vital for a healthy aquarium. Rich plants and vegetation will helps also to ensure a safety barrier for maintaining a lower toxicity level in your aquarium.

Plants can be fixed and/or floating. If this is your first aquarium you may find it easier to have a selection of fixed plants before trying floating plants. Floating plants are beautiful but they do have a tendency to collect debris, which can make it more difficult to clean.

Of course, you could also choose artificial plants if you would like. There are numerous advantages to artificial plants, including the fact that you never have to worry about trimming them, they are easy to clean and they will never die. Most have a base that allows them to be easily positioned to the bottom of the tank. How natural your artificial plants look will depend upon how much you spend.

Testing the Water

If you are serious about setting up an aquarium you will also need a kit for testing the water. This will help to ensure the pH-value of the water is properly maintained. There are many different types of water testing kits available on the market. Some are more advanced than others. There are some kits that can successfully measure levels of nitrate, ammonia and pH. A basic kit such as this should be sufficient for just starting out.

It should be kept in mind that the time when you are first introducing your fish to the aquarium is one of the most dangerous for your fish. During this time period, the beneficial bacteria that will help to detoxify the wastes in the water will not have fully developed yet. Biological filters can help with this later on, which may also cause the ammonia levels to peak. A peak within ammonia levels can be caused by dirty water with debris as well as adding medicines to the water or having a filter that is too small for the size of your tank.

You can also use a nitrate test kit for testing the nitrogen cycle. As a beginner, this kit will not be as essential but it will make it easier for you to know what is going on with your aquarium and help to prevent the possibility of your fish of dying from nitrate poisoning. At the end of the nitrogen cycle, nitrate levels will peak as the nitrate is near the end. When there are increased levels of nitrate, the situation becomes dangerous for the fish. If your water has an oily shimmer near the top, this can be an indicator that the nitrate levels are too high. If the nitrate levels are too high, it is critical for you to do several water changes. Increasing the aeration of the water can help as well.

A pH test kit is also important. It is imperative that you test the pH of your water before you actually buy your fish because the type of fish that you buy will depend upon the pH of your water. It should be noted that before your fish actually come to you they may have lived in a different pH than what you have in your tank and it is crucial to give them a chance to adapt to the new values. There are many types of fish that have special requirements regarding pH values and they may not be able to survive within your water even with time to adjust. You will need to either adjust the pH value in your tank to suit those fish or choose species of fish that will be able to thrive in your pH value water.

As a beginner you will find that most testing kits are actually fairly easy to use. The results of the test are based on color changes in samples of water that are taken and tested.

Setting up your Aquarium

Before you begin to actually fill up your aquarium, you will need to make sure it has been thoroughly cleaned to remove any contaminants, dust and dirt. You can use a small amount of dish detergent and warm water to clean the tank, but make sure you follow up right away with a rinse of hot water to remove any detergent from the surface. You may need to rinse several times. Absolutely no residue should be left as it can harm your fish.

The next step will be to wash all of the items that will go inside the aquarium. Start with your gravel. Wash it under running water. Do not use anything other than water. You can place it in a bucket but make sure that there have been no detergents or other solutions in the bucket. Stir the gravel around and continue changing out the water until it runs clear.

Next, wash all of the décor that will be placed in the aquarium. Wash each piece individually. If you plan to use an under gravel filtration system, be aware that you will also need to wash the plates before they are placed in the aquarium. Also, if you plan to use any natural materials, you should treat them before they are used. This can be done by soaking them in a solution of water and chlorine bleach. Rinse using fresh water and then soak them again in fresh water. Finally, dry them thoroughly to help prevent any undesirable elements such as parasites from being transferred into your aquarium.

When actually setting up the aquarium, make sure that the location you have selected has a completely flat floor and there will be no shaking. You might consider using some type of matting between the floor and the stand to help reduce the possibility of any unevenness. Prior to filling the aquarium, be sure that you have a water conditioner on hand that will remove chlorine from the water. Chlorine is added to tap water in many locales to kill microorganisms.

Start by testing the aquarium for leaks. While it may be tempting to skip over this step, it is recommended that you check first as leaks can be quire annoying and it can also be difficult to attempt to plug a leak once the tank has been filled. Fill the tank with tap water and leave it for several hours. If there are no indications of leaks, pump out the water and then rinse the tank. You can now add gravel to the bottom. If you are going to use an underwater gravel filter and plates you will need to put them into place prior to putting in the gravel. The gravel should be filled to a height of at least one inch and up to three inches.

When you are applying the gravel, make sure that it is sloped from back to front. The higher part of the slope should be toward the back to provide a better view. Fill about half of the aquarium with water. You may find it easier to direct the flow of water along the sides of the aquarium. Make sure you do this slowly and carefully to keep the tank clear. If your tank seems to be cloudy you can allow the water to rest for a day or so until particles and debris settle back to the bottom.

The next step is installing the thermometer, heater and filter. Keep in mind that you should water for awhile before you actually plug them in. At this point, you should only attach the equipment at suitable locations in the tank. The heater should be positioned in an area where the circulation of the water is at the highest point to help ensure an equal temperature throughout the tank.

You can also position your decorative material such as plastic plants and rock formations. These items should be fixed to the substrate so they will not float or topple over. Make sure you have washed each item before placing them in the tank. Take care to hide any accessories or tubes for the best view. You can also place any live materials in the tank at this point. Position them so that they will receive a good supply of oxygen.

Plants can be gently positioned into the substrate. Two excellent plans to consider are the Water Sprite and the Java Moss. Both are great for beginners. You might try letting them float in the water for a few days and giving them time to start developing roots; a process which takes about four days. You can then more easily attach the plants into the substrate. You can also use some heavier stones to place around the plants to more securely affix them to the substrate.

Keep in mind that plants should not be left to float on the surface for long as they may begin to grow in a strange shape and will not look quite right when you do affix them.

After the plants are in place, check to make sure you have not forgotten anything and then fill the aquarium full. Once the aquarium is full you can then start the heater. Keep the heater in the water for about thirty minutes before you actually turn it on. Make sure it is positioned so that you will be able to more easily read it. Always read the manufacturer's directions as different models can vary. After you have turned on the heater, you will need to monitor the water temperature for a day.

The next step will be to make sure you have proper aeration. When you use an air tube, there is a risk that the water will siphon back into the tube, particularly if the tubes are placed lower than the water, so it is important to make sure that the air pump is placed above water level.

Now, you can turn on the power or mechanical filtration if you are using one of these devices. Make sure the filter is set up so that the flow of water will be concentrated toward the center of the tank. Once you have plugged in the filter, let it run for a full day.

Remember that you should never shut off the filter except for short periods of time as needed for maintenance. The motor should not be allowed to run dry as it can become damaged. Also, if you turn the filter on and off it can unnecessary wear and tear and may cause toxins to build up inside the filter which can then be released into the water.

WATER CHEMISTRY
AND CONDITIONING

Due to the fact that your fish will spend their entire lives in water, the water is the most important element in your aquarium. In order to maintain a healthy aquarium, you must understand the water. There are three basic aspects to the water in your tank. They are the temperature, the pH and the levels of constituents that are present in the water.

Most tropical fish do best in warmer waters. They are quite hardy and can actually do fine in a wide range of temperatures, but warmer temperatures are best for tropical fish. This is why you must have a heater that can be controlled by a thermostat if you want to keep tropical fish. A thermometer that is easy to use will help you to better check and maintain the temperature of your water. The temperature of the water will also affect a variety of chemical and biological processes in the tank as well.

The pH value measures the acidity or alkalinity of a particular solution. The pH can range from 0 to 14. 0 is the most acidic and 14 is the most alkaline. Freshwater fish can survive in a range of pH values but the best value is one that is slightly acidic or about 6.5 to 7.5.

Another important factor is the hardness of the water. This refers to the amount of minerals that are dissolved in the water, particularly magnesium and calcium. In most instances you should be fine without needing to adjust the hardness of the water. If you have water that is too soft; however, it can cause problems in your aquarium. You can increase the hardness of the water by adding some crushed coral to the tank. Remember that this will also change the pH of the water as well; however.

Some of the more important elements that are present in your water are nitrates, nitrites, carbon dioxide and dissolved oxygen. All of these elements can be crucial to the health of your fish. The life of your aquarium can actually depend upon the dissolved oxygen within the water in your tank. Water absorbs gaseous oxygen. Turbulence along the surface of the water will increase the absorption of oxygen. Plants in your tank will give off oxygen during the photosynthesis process, but this oxygen will also be used up rather quickly. Plants also require oxygen for respiration and will consume some of the oxygen that they produce.

Due to the fact that all of the organisms in the tank use up the dissolved oxygen rather quickly, it will be necessary for you to ensure that your tank is well aerated. Plants alone will not always be able to provide enough oxygen for your aquarium, especially if you have a large population of fish. Also, it should be noted that plants that are decaying or unhealthy will also increase the oxygen demand even more. A simple aeration system will usually be sufficient for providing plenty of oxygen in your tank. You can also help to keep your tank healthy with regular water changes, removing rotting plant material promptly and vacuuming out waste.

Ammonia is produced by the metabolism of your fish and is then excreted through the gills of the fish and in the fish feces. Ammonia is further produced by the breakdown of plant material. It can be highly toxic and can even kill your fish if the levels of ammonia become too high.

Nitrites are formed when the ammonia is broken down by bacteria. Nitrites can also be dangerous to your fish in quantities that are too big. If your fish become exposed to too much nitrite they can become anemic and eventually die.

Nitrates are a nitrogen based compound that is produced when nitrite is broken down by bacteria. High levels of nitrates can also be toxic, but most species of fish are naturally more resilient to nitrate than nitrite and ammonia. The best course of action is to try to keep the levels of nitrite and ammonia in your tank at zero and the levels of nitrates fairly low. It can be almost impossible to completely eradicate nitrates in the tank, but you can help by making sure you do not overstock your tank and by not overfeeding your fish. Also, make sure your tank is kept clean.

Conditioning of the Water

Remember that you should never add fish to your aquarium immediately after you have filled it. You should allow plenty of time for the water to stabilize before you add the fish. This is because the water will contain some toxins from the chemical treatments which can be dangerous to your fish. You will need to neutralize the water first and allow ample opportunity for any dissolved gases to escape from the water.

Tap water is not a natural habitat for fish because it typically contains large amounts of chlorine that can harm your fish as well as plants. There are three methods that can be used for dechlorinating the water. One method is to aerate the water, which will allow the chlorine to be diffused into the air. You can do this by filtering the water for 24 hours. You can also use activated carbons to get rid of any chlorine in your water. Another option would be to add sodium thiosulfate to the water in your tank. This method will also help in getting rid of any trace amounts of ammonia that may be present.

It is essential that you take the time to research the types of fish species that you would like to add to your tank. This will help you tin determining the proper pH value of your water. Remember that neutral pH is 7.0. In most instances, tropical fish are able to survive in a range of different pH levels. Between 6.4 and 7.9 will be acceptable for a range of different fish, but if you know the pH value of your tap water it can be helpful. Where you live can influence the pH value of your tap water. Before you consider altering the pH of your water, you should take several factors into consideration. For example, if you have researched the fish species you plan to add to your tank, you will need to consider whether those fish are accustomed to a pH level that could be different than what is actually natural for them. A stable pH value will be more important than trying to reach precise levels.

Cycling

You will need to complete a final step before you can actually add fish to your tank. This is an extremely crucial important step so you should make sure you do not overlook it. The water in which your fish live is actually an entire ecosystem. In addition to your fish and plants, there are also other microorganisms that live in the water. All of the living organisms in your tank will produce waste which can become toxic. The good news is that they all work together to decompose this waste so that it will be beneficial for the entire habitat. If you can understand this you can take better care of your aquarium.

When your aquarium is just a few days or even a few weeks old, it will be at its most vulnerable. The water will be new and the microorganisms in that water could be toxic or beneficial. The main thing here is to minimize the amount of undesirable organisms while at the same time increasing the amount of beneficial bacteria. This is where the nitrogen cycle can be helpful.

Substances that are nitrogen based are the most common byproducts of decomposition. The nitrogen cycle is the process by which decomposition occurs. Nitrogenous waste products that are in your aquarium will break down first into ammonia, which can be toxic to your fish. If you use a test kit and it detects ammonia in your water, then you can safely assume the levels are too high for your fish.

Nitrifying bacteria are a type of microscopic organism that will assist the nitrogen cycle while converting harmful bacteria into nitrates, which are less harmful. Within nature there are numerous populations of such bacteria, but when you first establish your aquarium, this form of bacteria will only be present in small amounts in your water. A nitrifying bacteria colony will help tremendously in ensuring your aquarium's health. The phase during which this bacterium is being encouraged to develop is known as cycling.

There are certain conditions which are idea for growing nitrifying bacteria. They tend to grow well in conditions which have a rich supply of oxygen. Lesser amounts of sunlight can be established through less light and less heat, which is perfect for growing bacteria. As the nitrites become established, nitrates will begin to build up as well. During the second half of the nitrogen cycle, the nitrates will convert into nitrates. The nitrates are fairly harmless and are then converted into nitrogen gas which can escape into the air. Evaporation is not enough to get rid of all of the waste produced by your fish. You will also need to perform water changes frequently in order to ensure that the nitrate levels do not become too high for your fish.

The nitrogen cycle will begin as soon as ammonia is introduced to your aquarium. You can do this by adding natural plans. As the leaves fall off the plants, the first doses of nitrogen are supplied to your tank. You could also add a small pinch of flake food as well. Another option would be to use what are known as cycling fish. By adding in a couple of fish, such as Zebra Danios, you can help your aquarium to begin establishing those important nitrites.

Make sure that you do not over-feed your fish because this will ultimately result in having more ammonia released into the water, which can destroy the fragile balance of your tank. Be sure to use your test kit in order to stay on top of your nitrogen cycle. During the cycle, keep in mind that the nitrite levels will initially go up and then finally fall to zero. This process can take between two and six weeks. The speed at which the cycle completes will depend on your aquarium's temperature. You can begin adding fish within one to two weeks as your bacteria will have had enough time to become sufficiently established to support your fish. Just make certain that you never add fish to the tank if the nitrates or ammonia levels are still high. They should be completely non-detectable before you actually introduce fish to your tank.

Adding your Fish

Now, you are finally ready for the most exciting part of your new hobby; adding your fish. The type of fish that you select for your aquarium is completely personal but if you are a beginner, it is recommended to select a species that is hardy and durable. Fish are certainly interesting and beautiful, but those that are easy to care for are the best choice for beginners. Keep in mind that you should not try adding too many fish at one time.

If you try to introduce too many fish at one time it can cause a strain on your aquarium and the entire habitat. When you are introducing new fish to your aquarium, you are also introducing bacteria and ammonia into the water as well. If you do not do this slowly as well as in stages, the concentration of bacteria and ammonia can be too high and could be dangerous to your fish. You must also make sure you are fully aware of the species of fish that you introduce to your aquarium and their compatibility regarding other fish. Various types of fish are able to thrive in differing conditions. While it can be tempting to have a variety o f different types of fish, there are some combinations of species that do not get along well.

Try to focus on selecting fish that are accustomed to the type of water that you are able to provide. There are multiple ways that you can introduce fish to your tank. When you bring home fish, make sure you take care to only have a few fish per bag. If you have too many fish in a bag this can cause the ammonia level to rise within the water and the oxygen level to drop. You should also keep in mind that when bringing home fish in a smaller bag, there can be drastic temperature fluctuations in the water. As a result, you should plan to avoid exposing the bag to cold or heat. Make sure you plan your trip to the pet store in advance to help reduce the shock and stress that your new will be subjected to. Whenever possible try to bring your fish home immediately.

When you arrive home, take the bag and place it in the aquarium and allow it to float for about 15 minutes. This will provide an opportunity for the temperature in the bag to become equalized to the temperature within your tank. After this, you should add about one cup of water from your tank into the bag and then wait another 15 minutes. Now, repeat this procedure again four to five times before you release your fish. Keep in mind that you should never place the water that came from the store in your tank as it could contain parasites, diseases or other dangerous elements.

There are also a few things to keep in mind when transferring your fish into your aquarium. Try not to use your hands while actually transferring the fish. Instead, use a net to move them gently into the tank. Also, avoid placing all of the fish in the tank at the same time. Transfer one fish at a time and wait about 15 or 20 minutes before you add a new fish. If you already have some fish in the tank, make sure you have fed them before you begin transferring the new fish into the tank. This will ensure that your new fish will remain safe from possible curiosity of the existing fish.

In determining how many fish you should add at one time or have in your tank, you should consider the size of your tank. The basic rule of thumb is that you should have about one inch of fish for each gallon of water. Remember that fish that are territorial will require more space. You should also consider common behavior patterns such as swimming and schooling for the fish species you plan to have. Also, keep in mind that fish that are taller will need more vertical space.

One of the more common reasons for some fish to die after a few days is aggression as a result of lack of space. If you place a few fish that are fast swimming in a small aquarium, there will not be enough room for free swimming. As a result, some fish can become aggressive when they are contained inside a small space.

Fish compatibility is also extremely important when choosing your fish. Remember that not all types of fish get along well. Also, all fish colonies have a certain pecking order. This is usually a dominant male that is then followed by a dominant female. When you introduce new fish, the pecking order will completely change. The fish that are already in the aquarium will usually have established behavior patterns and any new fish must adapt to those patterns. If there is a threat perceived to the order, the existing fish may harm the new fish. Therefore, it is important to always try to buy a full school of fish at once and to try and avoid any unnecessary territorial disputes.

Adhering to the following guidelines will help to ensure your aquarium is kept healthy:

- Make sure you check the aquarium daily to ensure there are no dead fish. If there are any dead fish, remove them promptly as they can spread infection.

- Each week, take care to clean out any decorations and plants in your aquarium. Trim live plants and cut away any parts that are decaying.

- Scrape away algae that may have formed on the glass.

- Check the filters to make sure they are working properly.

- Partially change the water about every one to two weeks. This will help to reduce the amount of algae and debris within the water. You can do this by using a siphon.

- Check your fish to see if there are any symptoms of stress.

COPING WITH PROBLEMS

Fish can be subjected to stress for a variety of different reasons. When fish become stressed they can become weak and their immunity can be reduced, which can make them susceptible to disease. Stress can also result in your fish not feeding as they should. Breeding is also greatly reduced in fish that are stressed. Over time, when fish are too stressed they can become ill and die. This is why it is essential for you to understand the reasons for stress within your aquarium.

Stress can be dependent upon the species of your fish. Some species of fish will thrive in an environment that might cause other fish to become weak. For instance, if you have hard tap water, you should try to have fish that will do well in such conditions or change the conditions of the water before introducing fish to your tank. Another common cause for stress is a pH value that is unstable or unsuitable. Some fish can be quite sensitive to changes in PH while others are not susceptible at all. Always take the time to research the species of fish that you plan to have so that you can find out the pH value and span in which they will do well. In addition, you should find out the pH value of the water that the fish have previously lived in prior to purchasing them so that you can avoid any rapid changes when you bring them home.

As previously mentioned, increase ammonia levels as well as levels of nitrates and nitrites can result in stress. You will need a test kit to monitor these levels. Other factors that can contribute to stress include salt. Some species of fish are not able to tolerate salt at all. Generally speaking, fish which either have small scales or no scales are not able to tolerate salt water. You should only add salt to your water if all of the species in your tank can tolerate it.

In addition, water temperatures that are unsuitable or fluctuate can easily cause stress in your aquarium. Some fish do fine with cooler temperatures, while other fish must have tropical temperature conditions. You must take care when mixing species of fish so that all of your fish have about the same tolerance. Using a thermometer on a daily basis can help to ensure that the temperatures in your tank remain stable.

Additionally, the lack of physical space can also result in stress. Even fish that are normally peaceful can become territorial when they must fight for space.

The symptoms of stress in fish can be noticed by observing the behavior of your fish. You should continually observe the behavior of your fish. After a few days of observation you should notice that each species has a particular behavior pattern. For example, some fish will swim briskly while others will remain almost stationary. Other fish like to be near the surface while some fish will remain near the bottom. Any deviation from their normal behavior can be an indication of stress. You might also notice spots or nicks on the bodies of your fish that do not seem to be healing quickly.

Prevention is a much better approach than waiting until stress manifests in your aquarium. This is why it is important to make sure you are aware of how your fish behave so that you can help to ward off stress. The moment you notice any symptoms, take care to find out why your fish are stressed and remove the cause as soon as possible.

Solving Water Problems

One of the more common problems in aquariums is that the water may become cloudy, smelly or foamy. When there are such conditions present, the fish can be stressed. When you set up your aquarium, be aware that the water could be cloudy due to the grave being disturbed at the bottom. You can avoid this if you put the water in the tank properly. This type of problem should be resolved within a day or two.

If the water becomes foamy or cloudy after you have introduced your fish, the most likely reason is bacteria. When the aquarium is not cleaned regularly or thoroughly enough waste and debris can begin collecting within the water. Plants in your aquarium should be trimmed on a regular basis and any dead parts removed to ensure that the aquarium remains balanced.

Water that is smelly or foamy could indicate that there is too much debris in the tank. You can resolve this problem by changing small amounts of water each day. The best way to make sure that debris levels remain low is to perform weekly water changes. This will also assist in controlling levels of soluble waste. Wastes that become dissolved in the water can then be removed and cause bacteria to starve. Be aware that you should take care not to change too much water with each change to avoid harming the fish.

Also, excessive food can cause the water to become foamy as well. Remember that there is no need to give additional food to your fish. Any additional traces of food at the top of the water should be immediately removed. Check on a regular basis to ensure your filters are properly working.

Special Problems with Tropical Fish Aquariums

When keeping a tropical fish aquarium, there are a few things you should keep in mind. One of the most common mistakes that many beginners make is assuming that an aquarium that is small is easier to care for on that is larger. A beginner should always try to have a larger aquarium and save the smaller tanks for when they have more experience. A larger aquarium will have more water and that means that your fish will have more oxygen, space and less dissolved wastes.

Also, you can get by with partial water changes on a less frequent basis when you have a larger aquarium. A larger tank will be less prone to rapid changes in water chemistry and temperature than a smaller tank. In addition, when you have a small tank you must exercise more care in your selection of fish than if you have a larger tank. Some fish are territorial by nature while others tend to school. If you mix a variety of species in a small tank you are going to be more likely to have problems.

Another common problem is adding too many fish. You should always keep the nitrogen cycle in mind when you are establishing your aquarium. You must allow time for the microorganisms in your water to properly develop. Once the cycling process is complete, you should then only add one or two fishes to begin. Always make sure you give your fish plenty of time to adjust to their new environment slowly.

Over-feeding can be a problem as well. As previously mentioned, you should never over-feed your fish. If you feed your fish too much, the food that is not eaten can become deposited in the nooks and crannied of the tank. It can then pollute the water as well as consume oxygen.

You should base the amount of food that you give your fish on their body weight. Typically, one to two feedings per day will be sufficient. You should feed your fish five or six days per week.

Frequent water changes can help you to avoid a number of problems with your aquarium. You should try to change about 15% of your water on a weekly basis. Avoid changing out the water fully as this can cause you to loose too much beneficial bacteria, which can result in stress for your fish.

Caring for your Fish while you are on Vacation
Among the many different options for pets, fish are certainly the easiest to care for. Still, when you go on vacation, you will need to make certain plans to ensure that your aquarium remains in good condition while you are away.

First, you need to change the water a few days before you plan to leave. You should never change the water right before leaving. This will ensure that you are still there while your fish become acclimatized to the new water. Also, remember that it is best not to rely on friends or family to care for your fish, even if they are well meaning because most people do not know how much food to feed and will end up over-feeding the fish. If all the food is not eaten it will remain in the tank and contribute to the toxicity of the aquarium while you are not around to change the water. At the same time you should not give you feed extra fish before leaving as it will have the same results.

The best type of food to feed your fish while you are away is a time release block. This type of food is a bar that will slowly dissolve or can be fed upon by the fish. Keep in mind that this type of food is really best for fish such as Tetras that do not have a finicky appetite. If your aquarium has territorial fish, the dominant fish will likely eat the bar and keep the other fish away. The best option is to try these bars while you are still at home and can then monitor the fish. You should not attempt to rely on time release bars until you are certain they are suitable for your fish and aquarium.

Another option would be to use a mechanical feeder. A feeder is designed to provide flake or granular food and features a mechanism that can be set so that the fish will feed on predetermined times and in pre-established amounts. You will need to adjust the portion size so that it is suitable for your aquarium.

Remember that prior before leaving you will need to set the thermostat for the optimum temperature while you are away from home. If your home is closed up and the weather happens to be warm while you are away, it can be extremely dangerous for your fish.

Make sure that you do not add any new fish right before leaving to go on vacation as this can result in disaster. If you are planning to add new fish, wait until after you have returned from vacation.

CHOOSING YOUR FISH

Now that you have the basics of setting up a healthy aquarium, it is time to move on to discussing your selection of fish. This is certainly the most exciting part of beginning an aquarium, but it is not one that should be undertaken lightly. It can be quite tempting to choose some of the more brilliantly colored fish, but remember that there are numerous different species of fish and it is important that you choose the best fish for your needs, aquarium and experience. Your best choice as a beginner will be a species of fish that is hardy, adaptable and easy to feed. Also, you should look for a fish that is not too sensitive.

When you are shopping for fish, there are a few precautions that should be taken. Ideally, it is best if you have already decided on the species of fish you would like to buy before actually visiting the store. This will help you to avoid being swayed by some of the more exotic and delicate species of fish that might not be suitable for beginners. You should make sure that you take the time to review the adult sizes of the fish that you are planning to purchase so that you will know what to expect. This is especially important if you have a small aquarium because you certainly do not want your fish to outgrow the size of your tank.

It is important to ensure that the species of fish you are planning to purchase comes from good stock. Spend some time at the store examining the fish and look for the healthiest fish because these are the fish that you should plan to buy and take home. Avoid any fish that seem to be tired or gasping for air. Fish that appear to be unhealthy in the store will rarely recover once you get them home.

After you have located the fish that you would like to buy ask the salesman to remove them from the tank gently. The fish should be placed in a bag with a sufficient amount of water. Remember that the fish can become easily stressed because the bag is so much smaller than the tank so you should plan to bring your fish home as soon as possible. The temperature in the bag should be kept stable while you are traveling amount. You may need to reduce the amount of water in the bag to provide more oxygen and air if you are aware that there will be some time before you arrive home.

When you are just beginning, it is usually a good idea to stick with a small selecting of schooling fish. There are several species of Danio as well as Rasbora that do really well, especially for beginners. Between six and ten is a good idea to start out with. There are also several other species of fish that are hardy and good for a beginner:

- **Guppy**
  This species of fish has been domesticated for many years and are therefore an excellent choice for an aquarium. They are also fairly inexpensive. In addition, they are pretty and have a sociable temperament. In order for them to do well, you should plan to get between 4 and 6 fish because they are a schooling species.

- **Swordtails**

  This species of fish are very pretty and easily recognizable by the long point at the end of the tail. These fish are available in a variety of colors, such as deep red and vibrant orange. You should keep in mind that swordtails can be somewhat aggressive, especially the males. As a result, you should only plan to purchase one male and two or three females.

- **Platy**

  The platy are actually distant cousins of the swordtails, but they do not tend to be as aggressive. They are available in a variety of colors. They are a schooling fish, so you will need about half a dozen.

- **Molly**

  The molly is a popular fish that can be jet black, pure white or marbled. Mollies are peaceful and an excellent choice for beginners. In some instances, the males can be aggressive toward one another. You should only keep mollies if you have an aquarium with a pH that is above 7. Mollies prefer a small amount of salt in the water.

- **Barb**

  The barb is another popular option for beginners. They are a schooling fish that tend to swim rather fast. They are also easy to feed.

- **Danios**

  This is another species of fish that swims fairly fast. They are easy to feed and keep, which makes them ideal for beginners.

Community Aquariums

A community aquarium is one that has a large variety of different fish that are able to live together in harmony. The fish may even come from different areas of the world. The only rule here is that the fish must be compatible with one another and must be able to tolerate living in the same general conditions.

You should be aware that successfully maintaining this type of aquarium does require some advance planning. The goal of a community aquarium should be to offer an environment for all of the various species of fish that is free of stress, stable and healthy. Community aquariums are not always the best choice for beginners because they do require a lot of attention, effort and time. The best type of aquarium for a community aquarium is one that is large because it will allow you to accommodate more flora and fish.

In addition, it is easier to maintain a larger aquarium than one that is smaller. If you can afford to do so, it is best to keep an outside power filter and double fluorescent lights for this type of aquarium. In addition, you will also need a cover to ensure the fish do not jump out.

One of the trickiest parts of maintaining a community aquarium is making sure that you have correctly researched and selected the right fish that will be able to successfully co-exist. A healthy community aquarium should have a variety of different fish. Some fish that tend to do well in this type of aquarium include:

- Barbs and Rasboaras-keep in mind that not all fish are peaceful and some of these fish can actually grow quite big. The best options for a community aquarium are the Golden Barb, the Cherry Bar or the Harlequin.

- Corydoras Catfish-these are fairly peaceful fish that are relatively small in size. They tend to do well in a community aquarium. Other good options are Peppered Corydoras and the Bronze Cory.

- Danios-these fish are active and quite hardy. Good options from this species include the Zebra Danio, the Pearl Danio and the Leopard Danio.

- Dwarf Cichlids-these fish only grow up to around 5 centimeters in length and tend to be peaceful. They must have excellent water conditions and can become territorial during spawning. Good options include the Ram Cichlid and the Cockatoo Dwarf Cichlid.

- Guppy, Swordtail and Platy-these are popular options that can be easily bred and do well in a community aquarium.

- Loaches-these fish are good additions to almost any community aquarium. You should be aware that some species can be a bit aggressive, but most are peaceful. They tend to do best in groups of four to six or more. Good options include the Zebra Loach and the Clown Loach.

- Rainbow Fish-these are very active and colorful fish. Good options include the Dwarf Neon rainbow and the Banded Rainbow. Be aware that the younger fish are not that colorful but will become more attractive as they mature.

- Tetras-these fish can be a good addition to a community aquarium. Some good options include the Glowlight Tetra, the Neon Tetra and the Black Neon Tetra.

- Some fish that you may want to exercise care in regards to adding to your community aquarium due to their anti-social behavior include:

- Angelfish-the males can become aggressive during spawning and they often grow too big for a small aquarium with a community setting.

- Gouramis-they tend to be aggressive and territorial.

- Red Tailed Black Shark-they tend to be aggressive even with their own kind and can be territorial.

- Tiger Barb-they may be colorful but they are prone to nipping at the fins of other fish.

- Paddlefish, Fire Eel, Pacu, Red-Tailed Catfish and the South American Leaf Fish-some of these fish tend to grow quite large.

Remember that the number of fish as well as the types of fish that you choose for your community aquarium can be quite varied and large but should be based on solid research. A community aquarium that is well stocked can be beautiful.

UNDERSTANDING
FISH DISEASES

Your fish may be susceptible to a variety of different illnesses. Understanding and knowing how to look for the signs of various possible illnesses can help you to respond quickly and prevent the possible death of your fish.

Columnaris

The most common symptom of this disease is the presence of grayish white patches or marks on the body of the fish or around the mouth. The patches may appear first as threads. In addition, the fins of the fish may appear to show signs of deterioration. The gills can also become affected and may have sores appear. During the later stages of this disease, fish tend to clamp their fins close to the body rather than spreading them.

This disease is caused by bacteria and is often the result of poor water quality. The shock of being introduced to a new aquarium can also sometimes cause this disease to appear. The use of an anti-bacterial medication can help when treated early. If the disease progresses to the point that the internal organs are affected, antibiotics will be required.

Gill Disease

When a fish has gill disease, it may begin to swim rapidly but will not actually go anywhere. The fins will move rapidly and the fish may go to the surface of the tank to gasp for breath. In other cases, the fish may remain somewhat listless at the bottom of the tank. The gills typically become discolored and swollen. The most common cause of this disease is the presence of parasites, fungi and bacteria in the water. The water should be immediately treated. Dechlorinating, conditioning and frequently changing the water can help to prevent this disease. You may also need to add an anti-bacterial solution to the water.

Ick

When a fish has ick small grain-like spots appear on the body. This disease is also sometimes known as Ich or White Spot Disease. The fish may try rubbing itself on surfaces in the aquarium to relieve the itchiness that accompanies this disease. This disease is highly contagious and can spread to other fish in the tank. It should be noted that an outbreak of this disease can be extremely difficult to control if you do not catch it in the early stages. One of the most effective ways to treat this problem is to treat the water with salt. This should be done gradually. If you have sensitive fish, you should keep the salt to around five teaspoons per gallon. Otherwise, treat at up to eight teaspoons per gallon, gradually building up to that amount. You can also use special medication sold at most pet stores.

Dropsy

The most common symptom of this disease is an abdomen that is swollen. The fish's scales may also stand out in the swollen areas. Fish with this condition will lose their appetite and appear listless. Bacteria as well as various viruses can cause dropsy. Infected food can also be a problem. It should be noted that it is imperative to catch and treat this condition as early as possible because once it reaches the kidney, it is almost impossible to cure. Unfortunately, this condition is difficult to treat even when you do catch it early. The good news is that it is not highly infectious. If a fish dies, it should be removed immediately. There are various commercial remedies available at pet supply stores.

Fin Rot

As the name implies, the fins begin to rot in this condition. They may turn opaque and eventually develop streaks of blood. The deterioration of the fins may continue until the base of the fin is reached. The fish will die if this happens. This commonly occurs from stress. You can use commercially available anti-bacterial medications to treat this problem.

Fungal Infection

Aquariums always have some spores of fungus present. These spores can become infectious when a fish has skin or gills that are already damaged. A fungal infection is usually a secondary infection. The most common symptom is a growth on the body that is white and cottony in appearance. You can use an anti-fungal medication to help fight the infection.

Hole in the Head

In this condition, the fish develops small pits primarily in the head region. These pits are usually white in color and may also produce yellowish mucous. Fish with this condition may lose their color, become listless and stop feeding. This condition is caused by protozoa and is usually a secondary infection. Poor water quality or diet can cause the first infection. Fish with this condition should be isolated in a separate tank and treated using a medicated food or direct injection.

Pop Eye

The most common physical symptom of this disease is the enlargening of the fish's eye. It may look as though it is going to pop out of the body. The cause of this condition is bacteria.

Unfortunately, there is no universal cure for this condition. You can try isolating the fish and using a general anti-bacterial medication to treat the fish.

Cloudy Eye

In this condition, the eye may become so cloudy and white that the fish is actually unable to see. There can be many causes for this condition, including an increase in the number of parasites in the water. Other causes can include malnutrition, old age and severe stress. You will need to check the quality of the water and adjust it as necessary. Most fish will recover on their own within one to two weeks once the quality of the water is corrected.

Fish Lice

Sometimes fish can develop small white lice on the body. The fish may rub their bodies against surfaces in the tank to try to relieve itchiness. Sores and red spots may also develop on the body. The best way to treat this condition is to physically remove the lice from the fish using a set of tweezers. The substrate should be siphoned daily to get rid of any eggs. Medication may be needed for a heavy infestation.

Nematode Worms

In some cases, the fish may excrete small threadlike worms. Fish with this condition may become bloated and listless. Loss of appetite is also common. You can use an anti-worm medication to treat this condition. It should be noted that such worms can be common even in healthy fish, but if the fish are already weakened due to some other reason, it can become a serious problem.

Treating your Fish

Taking certain steps when treating your fish can help to eliminate the symptoms of conditions as well as the cause.

The first step is to diagnose the condition by observing your fish. Look for possible physical signs and behavior changes. The next step is to take what you have learned and begin eliminating possible causes for the symptoms observed. Check the environmental conditions, including ammonia, nitrate, nitrite, pH and oxygen levels. If everything is within optimal range, the next step is to determine whether there are any toxic substances in the water.

If the problem is determined to be water quality, you will need to change the water frequently and in small steps. If this does not appear to be the problem, you should then check the accessories in your aquarium such as the air pumps, heaters and filters to ensure they are working properly. It is also important to check whether there is possibly an aggressive fish in the tank that may have attacked the other fish.

Once you determine the cause of the problem, you should take steps immediately to correct the problem. Move any infected fish out of the tank and place them in a quarantine tank. Be sure that your quarantine aquarium is completely ready to receive the fish before removing them. The water in the quarantine tank should be changed daily with out 50% removed and changed on a daily basis. You may need to add medicine during the water changes. Keep in mind that depending on the problem, you may need to keep an ill fish isolate for about ten days until signs of improvement are shown. You should never move an infected fish back to the main aquarium until all signs of infection have diminished.

MAINTENANCE

Once your aquarium is established and running, it is time to turn your attention toward ensuring that it is properly maintained. A healthy aquarium does require ongoing maintenance but the good news is that if you handle it on a routine basis, it can be fairly easy and quick. On the other hand, if you do not handle the steps properly, it can quickly get out of hand.

Maintenance of your aquarium is essential. Remember, it is a living ecosystem that will generate a significant amount of waste and toxic materials on a day to day basis. Your fish give off ammonia and waste that can collect in the tank. In addition, the plants can also generate waste and will need to be pruned and cleaned regularly. The substrate in your aquarium will collect such waste materials and if you do not clean them out it can cause infection which can result in your fish becoming ill. Therefore, it is absolutely essential that you clean your tank on a regular basis to ensure that your aquarium remains in good condition. The following guide will walk you through the steps that need to be taken on a daily, weekly and monthly schedule to ensure that your fish remain healthy and happy.

Daily Routine

First, remember that you should check your aquarium and your fish each day. Look for signs of fish and/or disease in your fish. If you check your fish regularly you will be able to easily observe any changes in behavior that could indicate possible illness. Remember that speed is your ally. The faster that you are able to detect any possible signs of illness, the sooner you can begin to take care of it.

Any infection must be stopped within the initial stages in order to limit the possible resulting damages. Some signs of stress in your fish could include:

- *Clamped fins* - this can be a bad sign. If the fish are holding their fins close to their body and not moving them away, you will know that you need to treat your fish immediately.

- *Fast swimming in the same place* - some fish do swim very fast as a rule, but if they are staying in the same place, there is a problem. This behavior is known as shimmying. If you spot this early enough and take immediate action, you can cure your fish.

- *Sores* - always check for signs of sores on your fish. Sores can develop for a variety of reasons, such as fighting with other fish, scraping against items in the aquarium and due to disease. In many cases, the sores heal on their own, but the conditions of your aquarium are not optimal, the fish can become stressed and instead of healing the sores will become bigger. If you do not treat the problem, there is a risk of infection spreading.

- *White spots* - if your fish have white spots on the body these are known as ich spots. This is a fairly common disease that can be cured if treated early.

- *Fish at the bottom of the tank* - if you notice that your fish are near the bottom of the tank, this is an indication that something is seriously wrong. A fish that is near the bottom of the tank is likely exhausted and this is usually due to stress.

- *Rubbing on the sides of the tank* - when a fish rubs against the sides of the tank or on the décor in the tank, this behavior is known as glancing. The fish is itchy and is trying to relieve the itch. This can be caused by a variety of problems, including Ich.

- *Lack or loss of appetite* - this can be another bad sign. If your fish are not eating properly, you will know there is a problem.

- *Gasping for air* - when a fish appears to be hovering near the top of the aquarium, it may be gasping for air due to a lack of oxygen in the aquarium.

Ignoring the above symptoms can lead to more serious problems, which could cause you to lose your fish entirely. It is always better to address problems early on, when you still have a good chance of resolving them and saving your fish rather than trying to resolve such problems after

they have become more advanced.
Checking your Water

Remember that all of the aquatic life in your aquarium depends on the water. It absolutely must be kept as fresh and clean as possible. The chemistry is important as well. The nitrite, nitrate, ammonia and pH levels must be kept just right in order for your fish to do well. Always make sure that you check your water on a daily basis to ensure these levels are correct and to stave off any potential problems before they have a chance to develop.

Checking the Filter

In addition, you should check the filter on your aquarium. Keep in mind that the filter is responsible for filtering out the waste and toxic materials from your tank. You will need to clean mechanical filters every two to four weeks; possibly more often if any large debris becomes stuck inside it.

Feeding your Fish

Finally, you will need to feed your fish one to two times each day. Remember that you should not feed your fish more than they are able to consume within a few minutes at a time. Remove any uneaten food after ten minutes. Always check to make sure your fish are eating as they should as a lack or loss of appetite can indicate a serious problem.

Weekly Routine

When the water in your aquarium becomes stagnant, it should be partially changed. This should take place at least once a week and may need to be done twice per week. Large amounts of waste can quickly build up on the water and cause problems if left unchanged. By replacing a little of the water with new water you can reduce the total amount of waste concentration in your tank. Using regular water is the safest course of action as well as the least expensive way to detoxify your aquarium. If you have used any medications in your water recently, you will need to remove these as soon as you no longer need them. You should never leave any chemicals in your water.

A coulee of factors will determine how effective your water changes have been. They include how frequently you change the water and the percentage of water that you change each time. Anytime there is a dramatic change in the quality of your water, such as the temperature or the pH level, your fish can be subjected to stress. If the water in your tank has the same pH, temperature and hardness as the new water, then changing even up to 50% of the water each time should not cause your fish any undue stress. If there is an emergency, you may need to perform a large water change. If that is the case, it is better to do the water change than to allow your fish to remain in unsuitable conditions. If it should become necessary for you to perform a large water change, try to get replacement water that is as close to that of the water in the tank as possible.

In terms of how frequently you should change your water, be aware that if you change the water more often, you should use less water for each change. The longer the gap between water changes, the more stress your fish will be exposed to. You might try starting off with replacing about ¼ of the water for one week and then go from there. Remember that for a water change to be the most effective, you should take several factors into consideration, including the number of fish that you have in your tank at the time.

If you notice that there has been a significant change in the pH of your water, you may need to begin making more frequent changes with small quantities of water. Keep in mind that you should treat your water when you change it as well as condition the water. If you use water from the tap, always dechlorinate it before adding it to your tank.

Vacuuming the Substrate

On a weekly basis you should vacuum the substrate in your tank. This is extremely important as it will help to remove debris and dirt from the tank and prevent the wastes from breaking down even further into phosphates and nitrates. If your substrate consists of gravel, you should plunge the end of the siphon tube into the gravel in order to suck out the dirt. You may need to stir up the gravel just a bit as you siphon it to be sure that you are getting all of the debris. The gravel will go back into place once you have finished.

If you have a substrate of sand, you can use a clean garden hose that is about a half an inch or so above the surface of the water to help in removing any visible debris without actually disturbing the surface of the sand. If your aquarium contains a lot of plant life, you may find that vacuuming the substrate is more difficult because it can disturb the roots of the plant. This can easily damage the plants, so you will need to exercise care.

Monthly Routine

On a monthly basis you need to check the fluorescent lighting in your aquarium. Remember, the lighting is responsible for the heat in your aquarium and it is better to change it before it goes out and you suffer any problems. Many species of fish are not able to tolerate dramatic changes in water temperature.

You should also inspect the tubing and other equipment monthly to be sure they are in proper working order as well. At the same time, it is a good idea to check the expiration date on any supplies that you use with your aquarium, including test kits. If you continue to use supplies after the expiration date, you may not receive correct readings and that can put your aquarium at risk. This is also a good time to scrape the glass surface of your aquarium to remove any algae that may be present. You can use a special type of scrubber for this purpose.

Filtration

When it comes to filtration it is important to keep in mind that nitrite, nitrate and ammonia levels cannot actually be seen in the water. This is why you cannot rely solely on the appearance of your water to ensure that it is pure and safe for your fish. There can be millions of microorganisms present in water even when it is clear. This is why filtration is so important. Mechanical filtration works to remove any large particles of debris from your tank such as dying plant parts and uneaten food. Filtration makes it possible for these particles to be trapped and removed from your tank before they have a chance to decay.

In order for your mechanical filtration system to work as it should, you need to clean the material in the filter at least once a month and may need to clean it every two weeks. If you happen to live in an area that is prone to power outages, it is a good idea to invest in extra hardware because even a short power outage can create problems in your aquarium. When the power goes out, the first thing that happens is the shut down of the mechanical filtration system. Within just a few short hours, the ammonia and nitrate levels will begin to rise in your aquarium.

In addition, you will have to worry about problems such as lighting and heating. When this happens, it is always much better if you have an aquarium that is lightly stocked. An aquarium that is overstocked can be extremely vulnerable in such situations. A battery powered air pump can help during a power outage. In addition, you can use a sponge filter that will function off an air stone to ensure that the water in our tank will remain filtered and oxygenated.

If you believe that your power is going to be out for more than a few hours, there are several things that you will need to do.

- The first thing you should do is remove the top from the aquarium. This will help to introduce more air into the tank. If the room where your aquarium is located is cold, go ahead and leave the lid on because you do not want to add to the heating problems.

- You should also turn off or unplug all of the electrical equipment. It is likely that there could be starts of the power supply and you do not want your equipment to become damaged as a result of this.

- Go ahead and get the battery powered filtration system in place and running smoothly.

- Make sure that the water temperature is as consistent as possible. The top of the lid can be taken off to help reduce the heat in extreme heat, but remember to leave it on to help preserve the temperature if the weather is cold.

As you can see, maintenance of your aquarium is certainly an important issue. If you take the time to regularly and properly maintain your aquarium, it will help to greatly reduce the chores related to your aquarium and ensure that your fish remain healthy.

CONCLUSION

As you can see, maintaining a tropical fish aquarium can be a wonderful experience as well as a learning opportunity. In order to enjoy the most benefits from your experience, there are several important things you need to know, but these are all things that can be learned through experience and a willingness to find out more. Ensuring that your aquarium remains in optimal condition will also take some dedication and time on your part.

Through experience you will be better prepared to branch out and perhaps add even more exotic fish to your aquarium while still enjoying the many rewarding and peaceful benefits associated with keeping an aquarium.

To your Success!